The FOOTBALL Coach

Written by Jonny Zucker

Illustrated by Jonatronix

OXFORD
UNIVERSITY PRESS

OXFORD
UNIVERSITY PRESS

Great Clarendon Street, Oxford, OX2 6DP, United Kingdom

Oxford University Press is a department of the University of Oxford. It furthers the University's objective of excellence in research, scholarship, and education by publishing worldwide. Oxford is a registered trade mark of Oxford University Press in the UK and in certain other countries

British Library Cataloguing in Publication Data
Data available

ISBN: 978-0-19-835661-5

10 9 8 7 6 5 4 3

Paper used in the production of this book is a natural, recyclable product made from wood grown in sustainable forests. The manufacturing process conforms to the environmental regulations of the country of origin.

Printed in China by Leo Paper Products Ltd

Acknowledgements

Series Advisor: Nikki Gamble
Illustrated by Jonatronix
Designed by
Caitlin Ziegler

Chapter 1

Like everyone else at school, Jack collected 'Top Goal' football trading cards. He had more cards than anyone, even his best friend, Nick.

But there was one card that Jack didn't have –

City United's **Matt Denton gold star** card.

Everyone wanted the Matt Denton gold star card but nobody had it. Jack dreamed about this card.

Matt Denton

"You have lots of football cards," sneered Kev,
"but you can't *play* football. You'll never make the school
team at the trial next week."

"Yes I will!" snapped Jack. "I want
to play as striker."

"That's ridiculous!" laughed Kev.
"The striker position is mine!"

On the way home, Jack bought a new pack of cards.
He eagerly ripped it open, fumbling through the cards until ...
he suddenly saw the Matt Denton gold star card!

It sparkled in the sunlight.

Matt Denton

Jack gazed in awe at the card. Suddenly, the picture said, "Hi, I'm Matt Denton. What's your name?"

"I ... I ... I'm Jack," stuttered Jack.

On the card, the picture of Matt Denton picked up a football and started juggling it with his feet, knees and head.

Jack couldn't believe it. The Matt Denton card had *talked* to him! And now it was playing football!

Chapter 2

"I wish I was as good at football as you, Matt!" sighed Jack. "I want to play as striker for my school team but Kev is way better than me. And he's really mean."

On the card, Denton balanced the ball on his shoulder. "Would you like some extra coaching?" he asked.

"From *you*?" gasped Jack.

"It will help you become a better player," grinned Denton. "Trust me."

"YES!" cried Jack.

Later that day in Jack's garden, the training began.

"Pass the ball to that tree and, when it bounces back, pass it to that other tree," called Denton from the card.

After an hour, Jack's passing was improving. Then they worked on heading and shooting until it got dark. Jack thanked Denton and put the card away safely.

"Who were you
talking to outside?"
asked Jack's mum
at dinner.
"Er, nobody,
Mum!" said Jack.

Over the next few days,
Denton taught Jack how
to trap the ball,

back-heel it,

and take shots using both
feet. Jack was improving
by the minute.

Jack told nobody about the extra training or his special
card — he always kept the card hidden in his school bag.

Everyone at school noticed Jack's improved football skills, especially Nick.

"You'll still never make the team," jeered Kev.

"Yeah, yeah," said a voice from inside Jack's bag. Luckily, Kev didn't hear it.

Later, Nick asked Jack how he was getting so much better at football.

"I've been practising every day," replied Jack. "I'll show you some new skills."

Jack trained with Nick for the rest of lunchtime.

Chapter 3

Jack was still worried. With Kev around, could he really get a place on the team?

"Forget about Kev," said Denton. "Let's practise in the park today," he suggested. "I'm going to teach you something that will help you score *incredible* goals."

"What is it?" asked Jack.
"It's called a half-volley,"
replied Denton.

"Throw the ball into the air and then kick it a split second after it bounces," said Denton. "I've scored loads of half-volleys for City United."

"I've seen you do them on TV!" exclaimed Jack, picking up the ball and hurling it into the air. Jack watched the ball bounce and then kicked it hard.

Matt Denton

It took forty-five minutes of practice but Jack finally started smashing the ball into the goal.

"Great stuff!" cheered Denton. "If you do half-volleys like that, *you* could end up playing for City United!"

The next morning, Jack found Kev rummaging around in his bag.

"Jack's got the Matt Denton gold star card!" shouted Kev, waving it above his head.

"Give that back!" cried Jack.

Kev ran off with the card, laughing. Jack raced after him.

"Stop it, Kev!" yelled Nick.

Suddenly, Kev tore the Matt Denton card in half and threw the pieces in the air.

Jack dived onto the ground and picked it up. Both halves were completely motionless.

Jack felt like crying – he'd lost his awesome football coach!

Chapter 4

Jack raced home and frantically stuck the card back together. For a moment nothing happened. Then there was movement. Denton groaned and stretched slowly. "It feels good to be back in one piece!" he said.

That afternoon, Denton worked with Jack on long shots and dribbling.

"I really hope I've practised enough to make the team," said Jack.

"Just do your best," replied Denton.

"Were you talking to me?" asked Jack's mum through an open window.

"No," answered Jack nervously. "I was just doing some maths out loud."

The day of the trial arrived. Jack quickly ate breakfast, grabbed his football bag and dashed to school. He was keeping the Matt Denton gold star card close to him in his jacket pocket.

At lunchtime, Nick said to Jack, "Maybe Kev's right and we shouldn't go to the trial."

"We've got as much right to be there as he has," said Jack firmly.

Nick nodded but he didn't look convinced.

After school, Jack quickly got changed and then pulled out the Matt Denton gold star card.

"Any last-minute advice?" asked Jack.

"Just do your best," replied Denton. "*Trust me.*"

"Why have you two bothered to turn up?" snarled Kev as Jack and Nick walked onto the pitch. "You're both *hopeless!*"

"Is everything OK over here?" asked Miss Cruz, the school football coach.

"Everything's fine," replied Kev, giving Jack and Nick a dirty look.

★ Chapter 5 ★

Jack put his jacket beside one of the goals and made sure the Matt Denton card was safe. Then the trial began.

It started off terribly for Jack – he missed two easy chances at goal. It got worse for Nick – he scored an own goal.

Jack was feeling miserable. Time was running out. Then, suddenly, his goalkeeper whacked the ball straight towards him. Jack raced to the ball but he could hear defenders running after him. What should he do?

"Hit it on the half-volley!" shouted a voice from somewhere near the goal.

The ball hit the ground and a second later Jack struck it as hard as he could. His half-volley smashed into the back of the net!

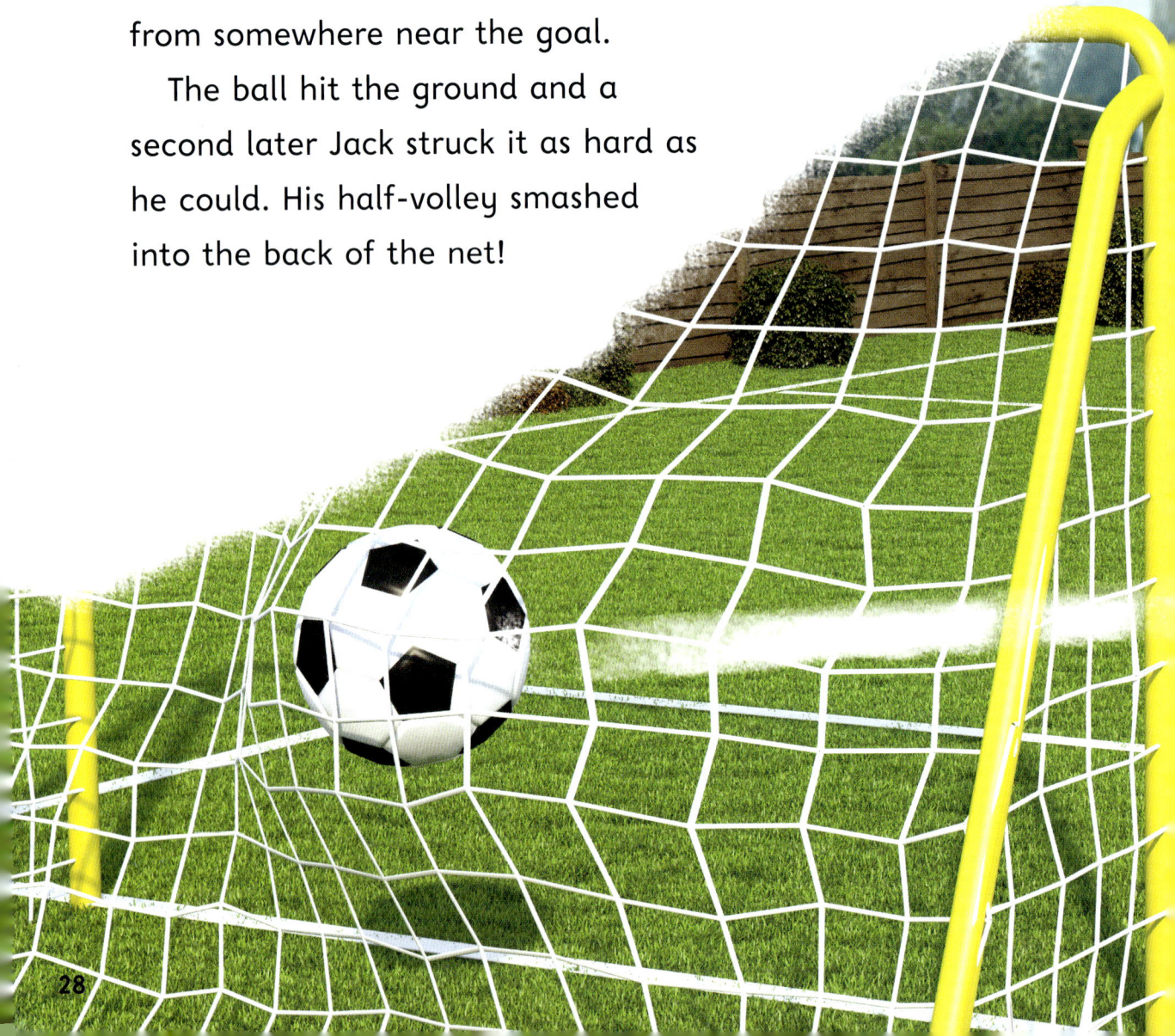

"Great goal, Jack!" shouted Miss Cruz.
"You've just earned your place on the
team as our **striker!**"

Jack beamed.
Kev scowled.
The trial was over.

Jack opened his bag and found Denton leaping and cheering. "You did it, Jack! *Well done!*"

"Thanks." Jack smiled gratefully. "I couldn't have done it without you."

"Jack! Jack! Jack!" chanted Denton.

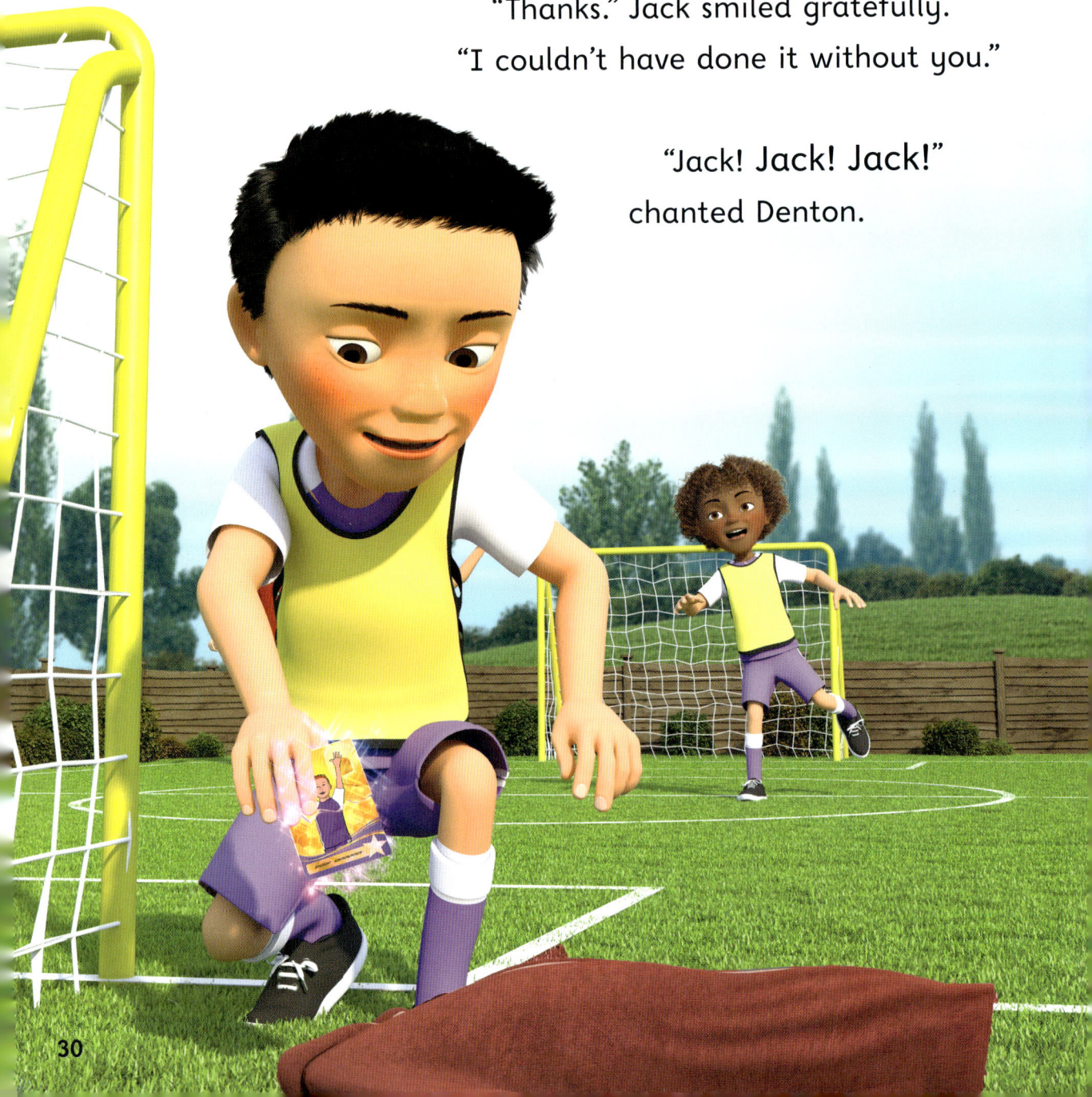

"Was that you chanting your own name?" Miss Cruz asked Jack.

"Yes," Jack quickly nodded. "I'm excited about making the team."

As Jack left school, he saw Nick standing at the bus stop, looking upset. He handed Nick the Matt Denton gold star card.

"What's this for?" asked Nick.

"It will help you become a better player," grinned Jack. "Trust me."